Memories of the Past

by Chloe Isabelle Morris

FROM THE DESK OF
GITTE
BLOOM, M.D.

Memories of the Past

Chloe Isabelle Morris

MILL CITY PRESS

Mill City Press, Inc.
2301 Lucien Way #415
Maitland, FL 32751
407·339·4217
www.millcitypress.net

Printed in the United States of America.

ISBN-13: 978-1-54564-253-5

Mommy Loves Nature

Mom is like Colors

Mommy oh mommy,

you are like a rose,

your lips so red,

your eyes so brown,

you shine so bright

that you glow.

Your skin,

the same as mine.

Sunrise and Sunset

Mommy, Papa, Chloe & Athena

In the clouds

I see my family,

Mama, Papa, Chloe, & Athena too!

I wish she was here

right next to me.

Athena would love her as much as gold.

A family of wonder,

and lots more.

A family with color,

joy with love.

Papa, Mama, and Athena too!

I love you so much!

New Year's Day, Christmas, and more!

Love you with care.

Family and Friends

Growing up with Mama

Once I was a baby,

my Mommy gave me her milk,

sang beautiful songs,

read books in russian and english.

When I was 2,

Mommy helped me walk,

played games,

and lots of other things.

When I was 4,

I started school,

but still had time to play with Mommy.

When I was 7,

I had fun with Mommy,

but when I started second grade,

she D-I-E-D!

Gods and Goddesses

Before living things there were gods and goddesses.

They tried to create life. It was hard, but they tried.

The only thing the goddess, Angel, made was more gods and goddesses.

Two years later, Angel, and the god, Saint, married on December 31, 1740.

Angel gave birth to a healthy baby girl.

They couldn't come up with a name then.

Saint thought of a name.

"We will name the baby Isla!"

Angel was so pleased that she made seven planets.

Last Day of Mommy

Poem for Mommy

Mommy is a girl that cares,

she shines very bright,

she is my Mommy.

Her eyes are brown,

her hair is black,

curly and short.

She loves to eat

fruit and vegetables.

The only Mommy I ever wanted

was you.

Memories of the Past

Mommy like the Night

Mommy looks like a girl,

that grew with the night,

a girl that shines like stars.

She loves like the moon,

kissing you good night.

Her eyes are full of starlight,

her life is a beautiful sight.

Mommy and Me

Mommy and Me

Mommy and me,

lovely as songs,

a girl tall like trees,

a girl short

and tall like the wind.

We sway like flowers in the wind,

a girl like me is Mommy.

Mama & Papa

Mommy Oh Mommy

Mommy oh mommy,

I see you in the sky,

your face is

in the clouds,

I don't know why.

I love you,

I feel a sigh.

Mommy

Mommy

Mommy oh mommy,

you are red as a rose,

your eyes sparkle

like the stars

in the night sky.

The pictures

you make

are pretty as can be.

Your necklaces

you make

shimmer with color.

Your skin smells

like creamed roses.

Angel

Love is in the Air

I know

she is gone,

but BELIEVE,

Love her!

She is my MOMMY!

Love,

Love,

Love is in the air!

Look Up!

Try to See,

MOMMY!

Three of Us

Music and Art with Mommy

On Christmas,

we go to the theater

and watch

the

NUTCRACKER!

Mommy loves the act.

Sometimes,

I go to the museum

with Mommy.

Mommy and Me Watching the Nutcracker

Buying a Nutcracker

Baby, Me, and Mommy

When I was a little baby,

mommy took care of me.

She fed me milk,

sang me lullabies.

Drawing of Mama

Drawing of Me

Learning with Mama

I learned a lot

with mama.

Russian, so sweet to learn.

Walking and running,

so much fun!

Skipping and jumping,

so happy!

Swimming and playing piano,

so playful!

Princess of Winter

Time is Here and There

Time is here,

also there.

Nature is grass, trees, and flowers.

I live on dirt that looks nice.

My flower is magic.

Someone you love will come back,

a girl or a boy can come in a flower.

My candle is for my mom.

I have a kitten,

and a dad,

that live with me.

Mommy, Me, and Papa

Mommy as a Little Girl

Mommy lived in Russia,

she was a beautiful little girl.

My mom picked berries in the forest.

She wore pretty dresses.

Her favorite color

was pomegranate red.

She loves to draw,

and to help me.

Mama as Mulan

Starlight

Oh star up there,

where is she?

Tell me!

I need some help!

I work so hard,

I draw like magic,

and also you too.

I love you so much!

Please come down from up there!

Up, Up, Up There!

Starlight, Oh My Starlight!

Julia - Rosa - Kalantarova!

Starlight!

I know you're up there,

I love you!

I love you!

Dear my beloved mom, You are great! I love the meals you make. You have lovely ears, lips, nose, and hands to hug, lips to kiss me. You shine like the sun. You smile like a rose. Your eyes that twinkle like the night.

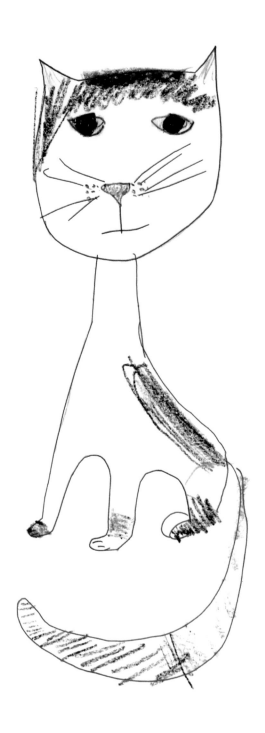

Athena Joins Family

CPSIA information can be obtained
at www.ICGtesting.com
Printed in the USA
LVIC05n0204041018
592357LV00003B/5